Nekyia

– Stride –

For Roger, with love

Nekyia

Rose Flint

NEKYIA
First edition 2003
© Rose Flint 2003
All rights reserved

ISBN 1 900152 89 4

Cover design by Neil Annat
Cover photo by Rupert Loydell

Acknowledgements
*Acumen, Bound Spiral, Fire, In the Red, The Interpreter's House,
Poetry Life, Poetry Review, Poetry Wales, The Poet's Voice,
Raindog, Scintilla, Tabla, Tears in the Fence.*

Published by
Stride Publications
11 Sylvan Road, Exeter
Devon EX4 6EW
England

www.stridebooks.co.uk

Contents

Ring of Water *7*
Waterglass *10*
Risk and the Heart *12*
Freeway *14*
Directions *16*
Blue City Angels *18*
Stop-Over Two *20*
Slow Dissolve into Leaf *22*
As We Speed *24*
Closing Time *26*
In Natural Light *28*
The Map is Always Palimpsest *29*
Sleight of Hand *31*
Ravine *33*
Hotel on the Edge *35*
The Ballroom *37*
In the Slipstream *39*
Video Game *41*
Water, the Body, Vision *42*
Prayer for Remembering the Blackbird *44*
Vital *46*
Red Sky *50*
Spores and Clusters *52*
Forest Fire *54*
Hotel with a View *56*
Quarry *58*
At the Source *60*

Journey Over Blossoming Stones *62*

River Questioning *63*

Whalesong *65*

Fetched Up *66*

Time's Feast *68*

The Blue Gate *69*

Rain and Fire *76*

Half-Deer *78*

Place of Departure *79*

Written in the Charts *82*

In the Mouth of the Shell *84*

Island of Snow *86*

Birdhouse *87*

False Summerlands *88*

Selky *89*

Blue *90*

Black Moon *92*

Selkies *93*

Island of Spoken Hours *95*

Horse and the Word *96*

Feng Shui for Nightmares *97*

Going Under *99*

Dreaming the Well *101*

Storm *103*

The Light Falling *104*

Clear Water *106*

Haven *107*

The Third Deer *109*

Ring of Water

I saw you again, yesterday, fleetingly, from the train,
as I watched the land closing into shadow.
After this slow winter season of rain
the whole water-table has risen, so the evening
opening a little, let sudden light race like mercury
into unexpected shallows washing the seeded barley.
Waist-deep in new lagoons willows etched black lace
of root and branch on the sky's liquid glassy mirror
while the brimming river in its swollen loop
drew a freight of dusky clouds across the fields.

Water spilling a wild brief glitter everywhere,
even at the edge of night. Though much has changed
I recognised you by the leap I felt. The same
as when I saw the flood below the house, at Walford.
Never again will we see the like in our time
our neighbour told us, shaking her head at the marvel
– even though we'd seen it almost every Spring.
After storm, in a morning of delicate sun we'd wake
to find streams, brooks, rivulets, run-off gullies,
had all poured in a bright flood across the lane,
rushed through the bare quickthorn hedge
(panicking the sheep to higher ground)
to circle the burial mound, creating an island;
a quietness of lapping silver light
stealing the landscape from the kestrel and the lamb.
For miles the roads drowned shiningly.

We took the long way round, up the hill by Rose Cottage
and past the spangled peacocks at Candlemass, to school.
The water made us all buoyant with its extravagance;
now you are more finely drawn.

I miss you. This spring I have travelled up and down
the country, restless as a hunting fox, hungry
with an absence difficult to name, or own, something more
than a sense of home slid in between blurred images
of a low stone house, a curved road beyond the rainfall
on the darkening glass: reflections,
in a flash of water slipped from its leash to run
for a while in brilliance beneath the willow trees.

'the way back is deer breath on icy windows'
— Joy Harjo

Waterglass

Moonshine makes the window a glass of water that trembles
with stillness and light as if it can barely contain such things
even though it remembers rain-opals and tricks of mist.
But the window is only glass, too slight a thing to be impassioned
by beauty and moon-lucidity, this sheer pale silence
where planets fleck diamond, yellow, blue.

I sympathise with the glass window.
It was not asked if it would accept this nightly scouring,
searing of beauty or its desperate absence in red fume.
Maybe my gaze makes it harder for glass.
so I should push the window up out of my sight
and leave no unwilling defence between me and the wild moon,
because maybe its my link to the moon, and her pull
that sets up this tremor, straining the glass
to brimming, to breaking point.

I could push up the window and lean out over five floors
and the broken conservatory where tri-bladed ivy
first climbed unwantedly into our lives, knifing under the slates
and panes of glass, levering them aside like paper armour.
You wanted a vine to drip quickening grapes, a beanstalk vine
to take us out to Beyond, but the ruthless ivy claimed us
came seeking our pulpy, ruby hearts, winding up the inner self
of the house into our room of magenta
to tie us down to the four corners with its poisonous spice.

I could slip my wrist and lean out to catch the moon's lifeline
as she swings slowly past the nervous, and now dangerously
open window. I could slide out horizontally into the watery air,
skin chilled white by the lunar wind, silver nightdress in feathers;
for surely tonight sky is sea and the moon is sailing
and I could swim or fly away – enter the Sea of Serenity
or the Sea of Nectar, become milky and more and more shining,
a moon-thing, thin as glass, a vessel for trembling light.
I think it would feel like joy, like kisses, like mother-love
a perfect stillness. I would no longer need the journey,
I'd be home.

Would the lifeline hold if I hauled you out of your dreaming
into the swooping air? Or would I hover there like a white moth
caught by your light and the curve of your arm
as you turned in your sleep to comfort me?

Risk and the Heart

The year's inner hinge is opening towards the dark
and the cracks in the town are widening, allowing
a herd of dreams to come racing up from the marshes
under the city's heart. Some dreams are gentle teachers,
active in the last frail rays of the old sun, these
have a thoughtful dust-mote quality, a bee-dance memory;
we all become poignant in September.

Others grow spikes on their heels and come trampling in
with lies and a curt hardening. Last week
I saw a white deerskin stretched like a sheet
in a shop window: *Antiques and Curios* in fake Victorian,
the white deer's head and its nine tined antlers
gazing over the cigarettes cards,
the shelf full of chipped plaster Marys.

Now I never look that way; pass on the other side,
stepping over the crouching beggars and singers
my eyes low, my token coins like useless scraps of croissant
in this huge freezing wind. Winter wind that follows me home,
climbs numbingly into my body, enters the fires
so we sit on two sides of an ashy hearth, wondering
how we got caught in this place of flayed exhibits.
At night, I could weave a dozen nests for white owls
from the silver hairs I collect in brushfulls.

The dream of the deer goes on running into my sleep
drumming into my head, fusing into my heartbeats.
I can't find the deer's bones though I search
and search the windswept malls and terraces, listen
for its breath on the windows. Someone told me
it was severed to the Four Winds but once
in the river's quick reflection I saw its pearly ghost.
So real, I nearly stroked my hand down its back, or did so,
watching the leafy green of its eyes warm to me.

This morning, bee-dreams came. Faded now, they fell
like flakes of gold towards the shadow, dancing
a map within a shaft of early light. They know we are lost
here, and they tell me the way to get back home
is to risk the serpentine curves of the old road,
follow its flow of energy under the hill and leave
on the last of its breath. Go to the West: the deer's gift
of its white skin wrapped tightly around us for warmth.

Freeway

You once said (stranding my hair in ties
through your fingers)
we'd take a polished vintage car
with luggage strapped to the back and
travel slowly (as your lips once moved through
the labyrinth of my skin's channels, slow zone
to zone)
taste the mountain's crystal heart
in the mouth-aching, downhill rushing wind.

Move like sleepwalkers in love, savouring
the transition from one dream
or temporary destination, to another,

finding lanes where coloured horses pace us
beyond baulks of leafy oak and hazel

touching shrines to Mary or raggy bushes
overhanging holy Mother-springs

where with prayer and gentleness,
we would lay the inexplicably dead
found form of a white hart
on cornflower and woundwort.

We could sample viney local juices thick
with fantasies and I
could try to find the amber merchant
in her studio, while you drank yellow beer,
watching the angels swinging in and out
of the cathedral's *son et lumiere.*

This fast road eats my symbols.
Sometimes I see its eyes staring back
at our headlights. *Faster* it whispers
rain-slick on its surface like the greased hair
of a new god. *There is nothing
between the points of A and B. There is only
the beginning and the end, entrance and exit,
what you spill here are my dues: hearts and money
the dead eyes of a deer, clear air.*

I am sullen. At the motel I swallow cheap whisky
and allow the lights of the roads to blur,
tired eyes and sentiment seeing a long looping chain
of bryony poisoning the distance.

Directions

We are travelling through Autumn's worn edges,
keeping storm to the distant east, sky there
growls thundersteel and sulphur, snake clouds
circling a grey weather spiral.
Leaves scale the air, sometimes the road
is all leaves, a fractured whispering fragment.

Beneath the maps, our own lists and diagrams.
They read like the lines of my palm:
Karma, the gypsy said. *Here on the left,*
is what you were born with and here
on the right, on this inner skin
that waits like parchment, this is Darma:
how you travel your crossroads and choices.

Such vague scrawlings these wormy tracks and mazes.
Fretful, right over left I try to find
the paper version of the Mount of Venus;
it should be Paradise, journey's end.
If you take the frost lane west from winter's corner...

The nearer mountains are already white
and my blind fingers itch over the rough cartography
as if it were embossed with Braille directions
making all come clear by touch.

We continue to pretend we read sign language,
that we are not lost at the outer edge where
the Beasts come into the blue *(fire and water
dragons open-mouthed eat the four directions)*.

That the boat is waiting for us
within the curved harbour's two smooth horns,
that our charts are set for the course west;
that we will sail on the turn of the tide.

Blue City Angels

Come evening, the blue-winged angels gather
on the city's ceiling and arrange their limbs,
robes and feathers against the chill of dusk.
Mostly the roosting starlings are oblivious,
only one or two dream the angels as presences
which slit under their opaque eyelids
disturb sleep with light-glances,
make them wake crotechety or evangelical,
so they mutter to their families *look
there are angels amongst us, crouching wing-folded
on the crumbling parapets and ornamental chimneys!*
The birds flute and glitter in the last light,
their voices snagging on the cills and Regency eaves.
They are million, they sleep jostled and crooning,
doze and dream, wake to be soothed again,
*blue angels, their wings like ours signed
with constellations, starry zodiacs!*

The angels tuck their dark fabrics
close against a cold older than stone or this
easy-going winter. Blue slate and lapis feathered
they huncker down, lean into the wind-breaks
of fancy dormers, watch intently,
narrowed opal eyes sometimes dilating black as space.
From time to time, one falls out into sky,
an Acapulco diver, straight legged, wings horizontal,
hovering near motionless on turbulent blue-violet air

fifteen metres high above the street.
She balances the air with her wingtips as a hawk does,
allowing nightwind to comb across her body,
pass messages through the antennae of her hair, until
she knows the exact direction of desire, swoops
in a quick burn of light, the great muscle of her heart
in the strong curve of her ribcage, driving her on.
Thoughtful, urgent, accurate, angels go deep
into the crowded city, fill certain windows
with shadowed gold and open some dreamers
into shocked joy: blue angels come amongst us
with bodies like ours in grace, their faces beautiful,
their lips moving... *Listen, what are they saying?*
What is it they would tell us?

Stop-Over Two

First, a cut black iron horse dancing
in silhouette by the stone bridge
over the one-strand river.

Whooper swans in a line of nine
calling like a chain of sensible children
first to last and back again.
Magnolia grandiflora
shedding meringue flowers in the lane.
A woman trailing frail and sensuous red,
her chiffons dated as a certain high-heeled shoe.

Welcome for strangers in the room, and
as such, in these familiar well-used bodies
we do not touch.

Late, alone in bed after the hour of letting go
the moon slid into my hand on the pillow.
I curled my fingers around its comfort,
dreamed of the midnight mare so salt with sweat
I rode within your body
flooding joy.

Dawn: you told me you had dreamed
of hurling swans from your gloved wrist
like great hunting eagles cut from snow.
Their feathers fell in muslin drifts
that caught the last light's rose and lay
in flames beneath the ice.

Slow Dissolve into Leaf

You had come swerving too fast onto my private island
gunning the engine over the intricate bridges of ice
caught me up like a warrior racing for spoils
– no arguments – no breath there on the hot black leather
only white violets scenting the air.

                    And then we had fallen, headlong
into a valley like a crack between the worlds,
verdant and eldritch, rowan and green ilex for sky,
strong forest ropes of wild clematis to tangle us
quite helpless.

The car had begun to shiver and snort like some grotesque
boxy horse, shook itself apart – silver wheels, seals
and perspex, wrecked electricity spitting fire
as brittle fibreglass and resins flew dismembered
to the ferns. So – I had undressed quickly
wanting to balance whatever that howling dislocation
had brought with its stink and oils, its tarry meltdown
and dangers. I remained naked, waiting
in the wash of emerald light and you
had slowly walked to the centre of the smoking debris
and kicked it aside until you found the map. You
pointed: *here.*

I was dumb. *Here?*
Your fingers moved as if the map were orchestrated
and I could hear a blackbird begin, recognising
an early cone of light in the waking sentient East,
both near and beyond us.
My breasts ached for touch in the cool air, my skin white
as the core of the moon or a peeled withy curved
in a ring. To you I was as pliant. And as changeable.

Time passed as we watched the metals dissolve into leaf.
You were the map made music. I was the blackbird
and that place – although tricky and not what I imagined –
was a good enough way station and we had no transport
then, to take us to any of the four directions, or beyond.

As We Speed

Moon is an orange mouth
whistling stars to her heels,
they lope behind us as she keeps pace
or catches up on the high ground
under blue-black.
She sends a fawn, startled creature,
as sentinel, places the cat
in its snake-form by the ditch;
Dog-star grins from a blurred hawthorn
as we speed past.
She is setting these watchers in pockets
where headlights won't go,
where the road falls
again and again
steep into darkness.
At each dip I cling to these metal
bones fragile as Bird
who sings from the dead lichened
oak fingers signing out across space.
I sway, heart in my mouth,
will the road lose itself,
fall into nothing, flip
over the edge of light?
I could reach towards you for comfort
but you are driving, hands hard
on the wheel
and no moon in your lens.

Only the straight headlights
and the pools of darkness ahead,
as we crouch silent, separate
as travelling stars in the dark.

Closing Time

Now a unknown town without signs and rain
sleeting down, choking the few lights that totter
and skitter over the broken pavements.
Rain twisting its little million fists
into the thrown heaps of earth that rise
black skulls warning over the crossroads.
We shout and storm the years at each other,
and you beat the steering wheel with your hands
in fury: *you should leave me!* Or we are dumb.

Time is closing in on us and we race from the car
to the bar of travellers and miners.
Enter a round high room, where a crowd of drunks
jostle their maudlin shoulders, shuffle
through green-lit haze on the dune of the sawdust floor.
In the white foam of black beer, by their found tabs
and treasures they tell the road of tomorrow:
boasts, lies, escapes, trickeries.
The ceilidh is softening the edges, loosening the grip,
light spins in the frantic glitter of wet rings on wood
a knotwork of snakes interlacing, winding in on itself.

This town's odour is wicked, wind with a taste of death
and boredom, a coiled fog in the gut. Only whisky
wiill burn it away, and the only risk is remembering.
The men are narrow now to the grit-greys of the town,
its heaps and holes, huts of tight-lipped windows;
they bring up the silver in scraps of uncut money
nothing special now to pick from the earth's inner body.
They clean it in water which wives bring in their eyes
or glass chalices small as eggcups. Secretly, the women
offer libations in their torn handfuls of gardens.

The men hunch harder into their glass in the jade light,
push the hours down to the dregs
the lost tracks of their voices going up in smoke
to hang like mist from another country.
One miner, dark as mourning in his dyed skin
comes drunk to our table, stares at our faces
I'm a poet, he tells us, polite and articulate.
You must listen.
His eyes turn inward as he stands swaying, begins slowly:
A women walked through a deep forest where roe deer
drank from the pool and fox slept in a circle.
She was moving towards the time and beyond the time
when she would meet the rider coming under the leaves
on his horse as white, white, white as Mary's milk.

In Natural Light

Morning, not night under false electric gloss
nor the blind secrecy of darkness
but late, light morning, noon; stolen time

I am bare and jewelled and you in jeans still
and your lose white shirt.
(In Manet's *Dejeuner sur l'herbe* one woman
looks at you thoughtfully, she's not young
and she has chosen her nakedness. The men
staring, safe in their cloth suits
seem less than she: calm snake
of *frisson* under the sun, curious.)

In this natural light, our defiance
of radio news, cheap music, petrol air;
nothing shut out, lace only
at the open window and the street close.
No smoothing shadows on the reality of our bodies
growing older, nor the horrors of the turning world.
We keep our knowledge, memories, mourning, anger,
yet undermine the fearfullness of every day
with the power of this small political act of love.

The Map is Always Palimpsest

Perhaps this country becomes smaller
by each year of mine that flies past
down these motorways and clearways.
Roads as familiar to me now as my palm's
cartography, destiny's direction;
as if the map is complete enough to hold
within the delineation of my own two hands.

Travelling, now as often as not a certain
fall of light on land touches some remembrance.
Can you stop? I ask. *Please.*
I used to leave it, rush past,
go with the journey forward. Now I demand
a lingering in places where some word or action
marks the memoried intersection of time and earth.

We swerve aside the mainstream, pull in,
the car shivering as traffic flashes past.
Distant mountains lean into the late afternoon
darkening as the sky gathers deeper greys,
long spills of kindled gold. This close
to the heavy duty road the trees are skinned
with lead and sulphur and the verge is grimy,
tired ochres of last summer spiked above dull grits.

Once I took a barn owl off this road.
Little left of her. I'd seen one wing raised
and moving like a fan against the dust.
I'd driven past, blocked in by lorries
thundering too fast, too near, so my hands
gripped the wheel ferociously. *Flowerface.*
her curious bright mask all blood, bones
crushed and torn as used paper.
Now, she is here: in her ruined body on the tarmac,
in her spirit-house of meadowsweet, in the premonition
of snow's wing floating winter between the oaks.

The map elides into another landscape.
There is the fact of the owl – and there is
the movement through the pattern of the left palm
to the right and what is written there.
This was a lane, overhung by the oaks and dangerous
in the dark months with black ice slick in the shadow.
You spun the car here late one night, my arm
across your neck and our early kisses still
glittering around our bodies, hovering like sparks.
We could have hit the trees, turned over –
but nothing would have mattered, it was already heaven:
the white moon over the calm white land,
the frosted silence. The owl like a ghost.

Sleight of Hand

The variable of games:
two kingdom keys, one cold room
the dark track of your footsteps
        dissolving
                in snow.

                Air and darkness, flame.

Alone, the minutes drag.
   Moon in the mirror
grows owl-full and heavy,
flies to the ceiling's dead light and stays;
      sleep shuttering her eyelids.

                You enter perspectives
suddenly glinted and shifted by shadow,   find
      I am no homing dove to the hand.

Not here   in these white thighs
       nor the soft ruby mouth of a flower,
close smooth
to your roughness.

I am flying alone down a dark lane
    calling: *Find me, find me*
        follow my scent of flowers
      through the night
          and warm me
for winter is frosting the feathers
that fly in the cloak of my hair
    and it is cold here, cold.

Ravine

Cold mornings. Grey
flutters in under
blue lace rim where shadows
dive for the last darks
at the room's edge,
its severe ruled width and compass.

Did you make me of flowers once
on a delicate place
a ravine of light, white violets?

Now I am owl, twisty-head,
plucking the last shreds and sheets
of dreams up over my face.
Separate,
my body lies
long warm and marvellous
in its nest of white, night
coats it with the gloss of touch.

Above the ravine
I stand in a tattered jacket
holding the edges together
as winds merge over me.
Letting go, I could allow
these winds to unpick my seams
from the inside out
parachute soft as a petal
all the way down.

At the Hotel on the Edge

At the Hotel on the Edge I woke
to find myself out, poised on the ledge beyond
the window, bare feet easy, strong toes gripping
the ornamental stone balustrade
six floors above the formal terraces
grey in the half light, black the elegance
of landscape to lake. No moon visible;
alabaster clouds and moths close,
sweet as scented white marshmallows.

I shuffled restlessly, allowing the wind to stroke
cool multiple breaths into my nightdress
that fluttered pale strips of gauzy ermine.
I turned my head right round, gazed over my shoulder
into our room called 'Meadowsweet.'
We lay asleep like twins joined at the hip,
you curled from me into yourself and I was so thin
I was hardly more than a ripple
under the cover's thick white blossom
deep as featherdown in starched green cotton grass.

But I am here, cold stepping a dangerous height,
out on a shelf of jutting stone, my hair lifting
like weed in a wave, skirt snapping
with wind that's shaking the mirrors so they shiver
like rain-silver leaves. Are you there?
Are you dreaming beside me down in the field of sleep

with its creamy florescence lulling over us both?
Is my body your warm shadow and heartbeat? Or
have you also gone absent, roamed away over the roofs?
Will you return soon, scented with moss
and pungent animal spices? Climb back into bed,
pausing only to pull your sleeping shape over yourself
and button it down, turn once to the window,
give a smile and a nod my way.

As I rock back and forth on my heels out here
in the rain, will the slim form of darkness beside you
turn and kiss you? Let her long black hair fall
over your face as her hands slide
into each familiar scintilla of your body.
She'd look at me like a cat, sympathizing
with the principality of night, rain's vibration,
the white talcy perfume of moths,
but would I recognise her eyes? And could she rise,
throw off the sheet, come walking towards me
with long strides through the room called Meadowsweet?
To shut the window between us, smile
as she places the grip of her hand on the curtain
that hangs ready to close out the night
from the heated room where milky flowers are budding
and breaking over the quilt and pillowslips?

The Ballroom

This is a house of too many rooms
and too many shadows.
 Long halls and deep recesses, rooms
for sleeping in furs and silk, for
sweet eating   dancing
                where echoes flash
across speckled mirrors
      and lodge in the flourishes
trumpets and carved flowers
      of fruitwood and gilding
framing French silvered glass
 gold flecked at the back

         the floor is empty
                 shines like a lake
         I could glide here
but the air rustles with too many
    feathers, too many claws
       and I am the bird
who beat at the midnight window
whose force starred white into black
 as it pierced
             and flung slow fragments
                 of knives into spaces
             between silver
and polished wood in the crack
      between one shallow breath

and another
white star breaking the glass
and the echo
flashing through rooms
mirrored in French
frames of carved and
gilded fruitwood.

In the Slipstream

What are we giving away here?
Is it only our nail parings, spittle
shit and black blood
that we give to the journey?
Our detritus, that flows from us
constantly, hair and sweat and skinscale
enough to fill pillowslips as with feathers.
All free given to the air
with our wildly flung perfumes and salts.

There is more. Each breath
(night-whisper
day-shout)
we give and give
to the journey (those words, their emotional
charge, their *frisson*, electricity, power).
The trail is deep and thick
behind us, collecting in the worn corners of mirrors,
in faded songs, in the rubble of old repeating dreams,
in the uncertainty of other people's memories.

We are so fluid, such changers,
what little ghosts follow in our slip-streams?
Yesterday-selves
catching up, crying,
save me, keep me, I am you, I am you –

They are liars. Don't let them in.
They are soft monsters,
and they own a massive, suffocating strength.

Video Game

On screen the road is fast and direct.
the instructions clear: stay in the spaces
given/ no deviation/ follow the line/
do not lose concentration/ achieve
winning/ be ruthless/ strong/ achieve
winning/ Do not burn/crash/die/ achieve
winning

Stay in the spaces given: there is nothing
beyond the white boundaries except
for a vague uniform greenness, an emptiness
brighter than emerald. Do not burn
with a flame of desire, or a hungry mouth
or a cryptic message of music. Do not lose
concentration on linear patterns, especially
these white lines burnt on the green.
Do not die in the fireball of bodies and metal
that flashes over the screen for a moment,
a single moment of high white light
and exhilaration. Be ruthless. Achieve winning.

Water, the Body, Vision

Black lake, sheer black mirror,
    July breathless on the mountain.

Only the dry possibilities of lizards
in the few stone markers where the well had been,
somewhere else its healing qualities.
No supplicants now entered that remoteness
to bathe their eyes and cure
a grey rim of vision; occlusion of the lens
exchanged for the clarion of light
ringing between air
and the bright curved surface of the lake.
That evening – the few small hawthorns in silhouette –
I found floating lilies: gilt stars
illumined by depths brackish with underlying peat.

How still lake water is and silken in July.
    When we swam, the lilies'
        thick stems curled round our limbs
           like tongues of water-horses
        dragging us deeper into the lake's shadowed throat.
    We rode each other, winding tendrils
in green reins along our leaping
   fish-white bodies,
       in one liquid kiss
the water closed into calmness
    above our heads,   black glass

                        where lilies in their yellow constellations
sushed and murmured into silence.
For hours we lay and slowly watched the stars.

This swimming pool is sharp with echoes
and reeking chlorined water pricks my skin.
Our mouths are aching, empty, the scratched perspex
of our masks protects our narrowed eyes
from the water's sharp ministration, filters only
a chaotic, blurred entanglement of lights.
Side by side we are moving blindly, but faster,
always faster within these straight cordoned lanes
where it is prohibited to touch or pause.

Prayer for Remembering the Blackbird

And sometimes all I can do
is skate over my own surface
   reflections frozen in ice

And sometimes my bones are runes
scattered in ocean's merciless tide
   and I am deciphered by water

              Sometimes
I fly so fast through the midnight forest
that my hair writes fine silver prayer flags
in the snatching hawthorns
             and I am naked. So naked.

And there are times when all I see is grey
and I have no memory of pearl or oyster. Then
      only the mist will speak to me

Sometimes there is no running in me
   there is no singing in me
   there is no loving in me
       and I am less than a leaf
   less than a leaf's winter lace
   so close am I to frost's roaring
       and sucking, frost's cold mouth opening.

And in these times, I must lie so;
let Time enfold me
into the journey.

    Only,   let me trust then
to Blackbird   waking the Sun.

Vital

Friday morning:

They sell everything short in this city,
put their thumbs in every measure, set in motion cheats
and tricks and scams like clicking bones
in each body of transaction. All the fantastic beasts of dream
here become faint ghosting on a screen, you see them
limping past dragging their wings; too thin to cast a shadow.

This morning at the market, between stalls of reddened meats,
the hallucinogens, the comics and cigarettes
I heard someone say: *Vital to me … vital …*

Friday night:

*Essential to me – my essence – without which
I do not live and know I am in death –*

This is a town of repossessions and theft,
pinched delicatessens, grimy launderettes.
Fathers and mothers here scrape a meagre living
the way deer scrape snow from moss;
their children are learning a new arithmetic,
selling sex as hard currency, looking for joy in the clubs
where cold water won't run. In rowdy midnight streets
they laugh at the crazy songs of the old mad woman
who croons loneliness out to the space of smoky crimson
where she says the stars are hidden.

*Where is the Sun, where is the Moon? Where is the lover
who courted my life all down the long west wind?*

We search the graffiti of heartbreak for a message:
Go This Way Out Of Here, or *Don't Look Back*
or *Enter my House and Be Glad* (a sanctuary,
someone playing the piano or an artist
filtering the water into washes of clean landscape).
This town has no skill with colour, the sun
has no aspect of yellow, the mountain
has lost all its blue longing and threatens like slag.

Malicious wind grits our eyes, pulls our hair,
mishandles our clothes so we flap and sway stupidly
lurch and lean and cling to each other for dear life
as we follow the dirty walkways beneath office blocks of steel
and sky-lit glass. These towers covet our breath
and heartbeats. Like everything else in this counterfeit town
they are hungry for blood and bone; they have no roots,
no access roads to the place of thunder and fire
where love is a vivid flower formed by the pulse
of two bodies on one single stem.

Saturday morning:

The old drunken busker drags herself up the hill,
left foot limping. The silver stall shakes with the pure sound
of her coloraturo, cymbals and castanets made of jugs
and Indian dishes splash light over stiff tarpaulins
breaking ice into strings of bells as she sings the street awake.
Last night, someone drew a whole frieze of horses
on the daubed concrete under the bridge.
Scraps of old statements sprayed on in red
become part of the flying hooves, names and emotions
were broken by line into speed and sinew
to form a new thunder and lightning.
If you press your face to the wall and close your eyes
you can feel hot grassy breath, restless shivering muscles.
Snatch the time: the horses won't stay.

This city could swallow us with her mouth of dust
and we'd become grains in the wind's collective howling.
Or we can find the pathways that lead us out and in,
whistle up our own private iconography of hound and hare
or deer, keep them with us like guardian angels
that we talk to every night. They'll be imaged on hoardings
and sweet wrappers, blazoned on jackets, used to sell beer
and cashmere suits. But wherever we find them
we'll re-collect them and let them run: every step vital.
We must whisper joy into the grey wind an atom at a time,
the winds carry everything they are given.

<u>Saturday night</u>:

*You are offering me pomegranates and last summer's pears.
What is bitter, what is sweet? Salt and sour and honey,
still in the dark of the city we can dream essential light
into each other's bodies, find the track that leads us home.*

Red Sky

There are many cities between us and the sea.
Travelling west, we watch them unfolding streets
like flowers at the blurred limits of horizon,
long stalks and twisty vines of walls
building up in bloomed cloud ahead of us,
roseate and tender and grand.
I assume they are sunset and thunder –
but I do not trust the weather here within this map
and suspect they may be banked visions of precipitation,
motions of dioxides arranging themselves
into glacial precincts, tall, many-storied tenements
or bubbled domes of sulphur where trapped words
repeat, repeat within miasma.
Are these the new way-stations:
The Carbon Monoxide Tower, The Nitrate Building,
The Bridge of Deadly Exhalation?

When we arrive (the road is straight, makes no detours,
no ring to bind or hold the energy within)
how will these fiery-tinted arcades seem to us?
Will we go hand in hand searching for the axle
that winds the cities out? Turns on such an endless rain
that falls in showers which sting our feet
as if we wade through venom.
Will we become as the bone-trees, falling into silence,
our lips pinned rictus,
and all that flows between us slowly dry?
Our shadows then becoming slow white stone.

Or will the promise hold? That beyond the evening
there are palaces of cinnabar and wafered amber,
good red roads and gates of ivory.
That there are mornings in cities when the wind
comes south blue as a gentian, coils so bright
that we drink it like water, mouth to mouth
pour it into each other's open throats,
breath becoming long wands of leaves, avenues
of sycamore and chestnut.

We were told this was a dangerous direction, and now
drawing closer to the distance, light becomes ambivalent.
In half dark we are entering either
the black rose of a hurricane or the first zone of night.

Spores and Clusters

As if the spores would secretly infill our brains
at night*: Do not leave the window open,*
> *the air here is dangerous,* they whisper;
> *can thicken the cells and spaces in the blood.*

People here cultivate velvet lawns, spend their evenings
in the bar discussing the eradication of moss
across bitters and vermouth. No one now
grows seakale or translucent berries.

Storm morning. You toss and turn, mumble,
as if something foreign had rooted its language
through your tongue and you must mouth into smoothness
the awkward textures and acidity of new words.
I force the window open, lean out to breathe
this unfamiliar sky where seagulls shriek for bread
across the leaden roofs.

The rainy street crawls with day-shift traffic.
A woman in a short green dress is screaming at the cars.
Bare arms and legs, hair slick as waterweed
she screams and beats her fists on shiny metal
Ford and Citron. As if these were her drums,
could relay her message, so
she beats on bonnets and windshields, on locked doors
inches away from men who hunch down in embarrassment
or jeer loud phrases measuring her breasts.

Some sit mute, grey as stone, others, impatient
to reach the safety of the factory's guarded gates
and landscaped acres – rev their engines
in flares of dirty smoke to drown her out.

I sense that all this is familiar, is replayed on other days
when the weather beats and breaks inside her head.
I try to collect her story from torn phrases that the gulls
leave drifting piecemeal through the rain
but her language belongs to this land and I am a stranger.

Only later, I understand
that she is the taste of these words in my mouth.
As if her voice carried a wind-born poison infecting
the solid dreams of the town, words in the idiom of air or water
lodging in sticks and bricks and stones;
as if her broken translations of jargon, statistic and loss
were the source of whatever clusters here in the shadows.
As if she were to blame for the fears that remain unspoken.

Forest Fire

By twenty I had carefully planted a whole forest
over that scar; a maze of new green saplings
on a hillside stripped to the bone.
I knew nothing of the wolfish nature of pine trees.
In my absence they must have grown an inch a minute
greedy to gobble the sky, branchy fangs reaching out
to tear the light, until they stood muscled and fed,
rank upon rank of tall repeated images of power.
I shrank into a lesserness,
something as frail and blown by fear
as the displaced hare or the windflower.

Now you enter this forest where black voiced storms
continually carve the same distorted glyphs
on every tree. *I am cold*, you say,
lifting the great two-handed saw
that was a legacy to both of us. *Do you remember,
how wood fires warm you twice?*

It is a dance to learn, this work with the saw,
it makes us both sweat, as we give and take
the fierce energy running its blade between us.
Each tree crashes into new space as fire leaps
to split each fallen carcass open, releasing years
of stolen memories, buried dreams; in the blaze
I recognise dragons, a kestrel rising, sparking
through the smoke.

Sun flashes in resins that bubble amber tears
out of the bark. I did not know there could be
such grace of myth, nor so much mourning in a tree.

Hotel with a View

Tuesday: I drag myself out of our heavy bed
and hurry to make it to breakfast. It is formal here,
severe as the hidebound chairs and conventions
of hallway tables. I suspect that Monday night leaked in
through some crack in the doubled glass, for our dreams
had a restless tint, something hardly remembered.
Easy to forget in this pleasing sensuality
of coffee, black cherry, cream
but uneasily I notice that winter has sidled up close
to the edges of doors and windows, is looking in
with pale burning eyes.

Under my feet the floor is so warm
that I curl my toes out of my shoes to cuddle
the tropical softness. I have a strong desire
to go down on all fours and snuffle the harsh scent
of this fire-coated creature below me.
I can hear its heartbeat, feel its breath
tremoring the pipes. I am a flea in this tawny-red fur
that rolls away through the corridors.

Outside the river is flecked with white wind
and the mountains are thundering.
The screens are active all day. We sit and stare our way up
all the glens and waterfalls. The view is magnificent.
We are given alternative seasons, and shown the rare
ring-tailed rodents as we listen to Beethoven softening

the cold glass of the walls. All is comfort; at each table
the balm of carnations and lace, pistachios, eau-de-vie.

We are almost silent, lazy and heavy,
lulled here in this room for ever adventuring
out on the clean rocky paths through the larches.
Those who stay for a while, go home with a fine knowledge:
we saw the whitethroated birds and heard them singing.
Also we found ring-tailed rodents and a rare blue gentian.
It is safe still, but hidden; you have to be guided
through hard terrain past feral goats and golden eagles.

There must be others who woke sweating
when the temperature faltered, dropped to zero
and mountain dreams slid through the silk-glove fit
of the scenic glazing, antlers splintering the frames,
spoor discolouring the soft red carpet that lies so still –
as if afraid that rain and the rising river
will release the ghosts of salmon out of the weir
where the last one leapt ten years ago.

Quarry

All night the road without signs
and rain sleeting around us.
I should read the maps but the light
is broken and the torch lost.
Sometimes words flash past, suddenly vivid:
Watch – Danger
but you press on, refuse to slow,
drive against the weather.

Until we come to a place where everything breaks
and the road falls sheer into nothing –
no hill
high bird

everything ends violently here, on the edge

and the fall

is carried in fragments of curlew and heather
south, to lie new,
linear, bound with white lines, signs, fierce light.

This mountain is blacker than starless night.
Our headlights cut across thickness of air full
of emptiness: ghosts of farmers and warriors,
wren, marten, honey-bee.

Hard knifing wind.
The mountain is strange to us, on this road
no shoulder to cry on. Only a seagull laments
in her harsh spirit-voice. *Not here, not here,
there is nothing here, nothing, nothing here.*

At the Source

The motorway finishes near here, or begins,
we'll come to its source, I said, imagining
black tar bubbling out of the earth
in a gravelly snake rivering away to the east.
Would someone have built a sheilding wall
as they would at a spring's birthplace?
Not sandstone or square cut oolite
but raw con-blocks, with a sodium light
as a candle to hold a driver's prayer.
Does St.Christopher travel the motorways?

Still you sleep beside me in the darkness.
My hands are gripping the wheel too tightly,
there's too much traffic, too much sleeting rain.
I am afraid to be part of this
deadly rush-hour avalanche, afraid I might fail.
I should be armoured, constructed of metals,
computers, striped bare of all abilities to
imagine, to feel, to sense Death's angels hovering
in these breathless inches between speed and certainty.

But the cab of the lorry coming up close beside me
is painted with forests. Oak leaves sway
by the windscreen, ivy clings to the door.
Deep in greenness, a stag stares out, his antlers
lifting the moon like a cup of light.
High in his travelling tree-house the driver

smiles down at me, pulls past
in a long powerful thundering, shaking the world.

Smoothly curving, the road arcs into four
points of the compass. Still you sleep,
your face soft, as if you dreamed of love.
Briefly, I touch your lips with my fingers
just to feel your breath.

Stars float out into the ragged sky above the road.
We are coming to the borderlands, beyond here
lies unfamiliar territory, another country
with its own signs and wonders. Another country
with its own language of the heart for us to learn.

Journey over Blossoming Stones
River Wye 1979

Near the outset, in the first fiery summer
we made the journey over unfamiliar maps
stones in our shoes and flowers
budding under our skin, our tongues closing together
over the names that spelled that early season
kingcup, birdsfoot trefoil, aaron's rod, monkey flower
yellow petals tumbling like kisses or confetti
and we were stumbling over a dry gold plain
– white sun and miles of light blinding the distance –
and found the great river's primal spring
in a thin vivid upwelling, spilled sudden crystal
divining the fertile winding
through ochre and granite and grassland to ocean.

      The water so small in my hands.
      Your hands over mind
      and your clear certainty:
that this was the source, the beginning, this
diamond flowing that ran through our fingers
becoming the river, shaping our lives,
holding us in its flood, sweeping us
into its days, its broad years, its beauty.

River Questioning

All this noise!
Shushing of water over rock
three sounds to it: first,
river's muscular run
down from the mountain's brown heather root,
from willow-beard north,
from earth's black mouth
opening. This is the river questioning
coming searching, helter-skeltering
roughing and pushing, pausing
to coil round the boulders
casting its form as a snake
sinuous rope
whipping the slick lizard stones or soothing
licking their sweet cool skins,
so eyelids quiver, squinting
green quartz gleam as they shift, settle deeper
into their thousand-year pitch, lean closer,
tongues rattling shale gold sharpness
where from, where from?
But there's no answer, no answer.

The second seeking? White water
falls and shivers
questions furled into veils of soprano, shrilling,
vibrating ice-resonance, frost frilled,
strung in a shine

at the water-stair's staccato descent, a snow-blare
over the rapids *where now, where
now?* through green weed caves under this route
this tricky time and stone crossing   tumbling and gabbing
and slapping
and still
still   Salmon swims sunwise under the hazel
snaps at mayflies starring the mirror-black circle
of the Well at the World's End.

Swans print swamped banks
with brushstrokes of Chinese script
leaving inquiring language under the alders.
Bone auguries slide in the swell
flat slates hold hexagrams written in shell,
a litter of oaksticks angular runes
– signs sure as a throw of dice – drift through divinations
on water's bright tabla rasa. Chattered interpretations
from mallard and heron syncopate with the drum
of the river's racing heart, the third sound pulsing, echoing
drumming this pulse of the water-race into the heart, echoing
where next, where next? Who knows? In cataract and ion
all river's questions flow into a cranebag of sand and spin
out to sea for Ocean to answer with a roar or a welcome:
with the rock of her two fists or her smooth shoulder to cry on.

Whalesong

Rain, rain –
The world disappears in water
and the car floats, glass silver-streamed, storm
entering with a wet mouth of thunder.

What did you see? Just then, beyond the windscreen
in that sudden drawn breath of weather?

*Only the sky darkening towards me
and something – memory or future? –
like the ominous presence of a whale,
a vast shadow*

shadow-whale in the sky, cloud-creature.

Whales remember the soul-song of water,
its ebb and flow, all that it writes on earth.
We are all water-beings. Rain falls through our veins
in long cycles of salt and sweet: deep sea memories,
patterns of stars coded into our genes.

We should break this aquarium.
Let our mouths fill with rain, let the whale's song
release these shoals that we carry;
let Ocean take them, she transforms
and births again all she is given.

This cold place of storms is only a passing season.

Fetched Up

Fetched up stranded in a breathless room
where walls lean in on us, their cracks alive with malice,
an oven-hot wash seeping in through the clamped floor
and sky in the one window burnt to a cindery orange.
Fifty past midnight and the bonhomie has altered,
the crowd at the bar are swirling round and round
in a swill of whisky and there's a whirlpool
in the well that opens inside this house
with a yawning sucking motion so we could all fall in
– you and I and the landlord, fairy lights,
optics and mirrors, sad men and the one-armed bandit –
the dark tarry stain on the ceiling closing time like a lid.

Leaving is like exiting quicksand. Words are hands
hooking into my skirt, their whole seethe and sway
following us in acrid smoke silting the stairs
and I can't see you for tears.
The men will murmur and laugh all night, sing on
when their throats are flecked with blood, dance
a round, as the house opens wider to swallow them down.

And we are fetched up, stranded in a breathless room
above the roaring household that vibrates every shape
of chair or bed or shadow. Somehow you sleep
turned away with your arm across your eyes. Beneath us
muted sound swells up in queasy waves and I am shivering
drowning or sleeping   dreaming or drifting
         in waves   sheer blackness   salt cold
  deep swell rippled with mercury light   skimming the crests
kissing the boat's brown oak –
                   Out here is great stillness
        On the ocean below the wheeling houses of the zodiac
      between every restless starlit wave is an abyss

I am atoms like the water. I am wildness like the light.

Time's Feast

Your face now is thinner, as if the years
starved towards the skull.

What would my hands seek
and hold in the long laden night
if you should go on disappearing?

You and I dancing on the table
slow waltz all alone
in a Marienbad landscape, cropped trees
of black and white.　　We floated,
light-stepping the spilled flutes and tulips,
the spoiled loaves, drew a whole dreaming
solace out of the rainy air.

Dawn – or some early hour of possibly false light –
somewhere beyond the blackout curtain
I thought you had risen, were standing
close to the door,
but it was Shadow, tense as the energy of Jupiter
trapped in a water-glass.

Love me. Don't be bones and riddles.
I am a cat of nine furs
to be stroked and fed,
you are gifted hands, perfect bread.

The Blue Gate

In this city of forgeries and unsafe hearths,
in the dead of winter
this falling weather
filling our throats with blame and threats,
icicles form glass points off eaves and streetlamps
as I stroke the neck of a wild swan
frosted rough with diamonds, her cold beak
biting the few crumbs in my blue hand.
You smash the ice with your fists
and throw the fragments like knives
all round the small arc of muddied grey water,
pavement, park bench; bright icicles cracked
and shattered, gone dull in the acrid yellow light.
You should wear them, you say, your voice raw
with the bitterness of this season.
Icicle earrings, cold enough for you!

I am afraid the swan will never fly
with this freight of salt packed between each barbule
of each white feather.
She will freeze to urban sculpture, motionless
beside me, a woman whose salted eyes
are frozen waterfalls.
I have become frail, brittle, wingless,
and who will come to me with apples in her hand,
honey loaves, a bowl of light? Who will warm me?
Will only night and winter claim me

as I lie immobilised beneath this anchorage of decay,
this heavy dust of dreams and failed desire?
Will I be as alone as the white owl
whose silent flexing swoop of snow
betrayed all youth
with the fading bloom of meadowsweet?

I am walking on ice.

No sky. Only the snow distance
a grey wrap over horizons, time. This is a place
of endless pallor, a leaching out; I do not know
if I am walking over water, air, or earth
only that I am naked, grey-blue with cold
my hair floating behind me in white filaments.
If I travel far enough, I will cross a threshold
for there are homes here
unseen in the whiteness of the wind.
But there are many dangers hidden in the ice;
they are named and horned
and wear the blackened tongue-protruding face, if
I walk into their claws of permafrost I could descend
into the cloud of sleep that lies a treacherous layer
below the water-table. There is nothing between
them and my bones except this flesh, its folds
and ancient scars, crevices of sourness, scales.

In shadow and snowflake the wind coalesces
into the half-shape of a woman approaching, gliding
over the ice towards me.
She is stooped with wing-weight, swan-headed,
long white neck curved towards me as we draw level
and pause. I see that her body is growing back
into its other being. Close feathering like downy fur
extends from her throat over her empty breasts,
across the wide slope of her hips to meet
the grizzled triangle of pubic hair.
Her thighs, unfeathered yet, are patterned white
with delicate ferns of hoar-frost.
Her body carries the marks of every year
since birth; not as tree rings, radiating outward,
but as circles tightening, spiralling inward
towards the spirit's cave. She was Swan Maiden
who gave away her feathered skin for love.
Now, as Grandmother Swan, she is beginning the return
to the whole owning of herself.

Standing before me she is familiar: she is Owl Woman
whose eyes see under the veil of the dark, whose wings
are silver shadow in midnight, whose wisdom is secret,
left-hand, healing.
She is one of the cackling Goosewomen, crones waiting
for ritual winter slaughter, swapping their hissing stories
of grief and joy; scurrilous, religious, brave.
She is White Bird Woman, her long grey hair
hanging in ropes for the children to climb
as she gathers their deaths to her heart.

Palms upward, she stretches her hands out towards me,
black bird-eyes intent.
She is holding pieces of ice and she strikes them together
slowly at first, then gathering speed
so they clash edgily, ring like bronze bells
over the ice-field: a call, a warning of breakage,
rupture, opening.
In the cold heart of her handfuls of ice
sparks flick scarlet snake-tongues that rise and grow,
so ice warms, whitefire on her palms, candles of crystal.
She draws the radiance into her body, lets it wander
the routes of her veins, the web of her cells
until she stands gilded, feathers on fire, sun in her skin.
Walking past me her feet melt bird-tracks on the snow.
She is going deeper, and at the point where distance
takes her, there is a spreading cloud of blue.

Swan stretches out her wings in thunderclaps
that throw the little terns into a nervous wheeling flight
marking out the circle of the pool
as if we stood within a shaken globe, a snowstorm glass.
She will not stay; beyond this mean distance
are pearl skies wide as morning, grey lakes
of ruffled silk where migrant birds come
flying down the compass from the midnight sun.
She remembers the scent of weed under water
and how cold waves of air above the winding rivers
fuse with her feathers so she becomes Air itself,
the great pulse of her wings, Air's heartbeat.

Beyond this winter is another country.
We are travelling slowly, sometimes
our heads are twisted round so we are gazing backwards,
our old lives seizing us: through salt to stone.
Sometimes we lose all sense of distance
and direction. Sometimes darkness floods our eyes,
so we become our shadows, cannot see
how near or far the Blue Gate lies
beyond the charted boundary of this makeshift city.

And what is cold in me is only fear.
Who will warm me?
Will only night and winter claim me?
Will I be alone as the white owl
whose flexing swoop of snow
fell, frozen
to the stillness of a stiffened bone, a stone bow?

In the thin ice of my round mirror
I tilt the lamp to light my face, take your hand
and move your fingers so they trace the lines
that lie like feathers circling my eyes.
This new-old face was always here, moving towards me
with the certainty of a bird flying in to its destination,
starring the glass with its presence, re-making
the last quarter of this white moon mask.
I move your hand down over these heavy breasts
slack and soft with memories of milk, down
across the deepness of my body's folds and scars,

all its planes of light and hollow shadowlands.
This is my swan-skin, my second-skin,
my own robe of feathers.
It has lain secretly growing, stiching its power
in the edge of every reflection, waiting
for me to claim it without regret. *Look, beloved,*
Time's changing us all; neither you nor I
have stayed as children under the wing. You too
have Time's feather-lines etched on your soul.

I remember the coldest winter when earth was frozen
to ice that stole the songs from birds and the breath
from deer and you and I found the vein of fire
running like molten crystal into the future.
I remember swans flying into our room,
their silvers breaking the hold of February
into shining pieces that entered our hearts like flame.
We are always returning to those white days
but there's no going back
only forward to find the way home.
In this city of dead hearths and blind alleys
we could lose ourselves in the maze, walk blindfold,
our fingers only brushing each other's warmth
as we stretch out our hands for some kind of guidance;
nothing enkindling our lives.

But beyond this uncertain horizon of secrets,
beyond this winter lies the gift of another country.
Beloved, *if we place our palms together*
our touch becomes a cup for fire's quiet embers
and if we breathe a kiss into each other's palm
the quickening of love will light us home –

Through night and winter, through ice and darkness,
through city streets and sorrow,
through separation, age and alteration,
always following these bird-tracks in the snow
towards the place where distance becomes
a spreading cloud of blue.

Rain and Fire

So you were called away and I am left restless
in the hiatus of this plain rented room.
Is the clock of the journey still going forward?
Even though you are absent are we still moving on?
Or have we lost the fused dream of future and memory?

Beloved, I am writing your name over and over
and my hand warms and trails fire
so I see the word that has come to mean
sun, heart, river, mirror
is a fiery script threading my book.

It is narrow here. The outside world
is dissolved in fine veiling rain
that murmurs a secret language under the streets.
If I listen beside the streaming gutters and channels
or under the eaves of the stooping houses
I can hear Rain re-telling the myths of the mountain:
of cloud-dragon, of white deer, of a rider
following the map of his hand through the forest,
All the myths are of love.
Sometimes the rain's song filters in through a window
and into a dream, so someone wakes
sweating, an unknown word like tears on their tongue:
ardent, primrose, beloved, forest –

Beloved, I write your name over and over,
before the lights go out, until it becomes a mantra
against the darkness of the daytime sky,
against the loneliness of sleep, against the terror of the road.

Half-Deer

All day I have been painting unknown figures
that stare out of my book
and worry me   with their right thoughts.

Rain falls in great bells of cloudburst
I can almost hear the rooftree
begin to crack
almost expect the sky to come down
bit by bit
infilling structures with this
weight   of grey cloudlight.

But the painted figures
hold up forbidding hands.

Except one in the shape of a half-deer
who is too thin, too slight,
too windleaf light
to be a power   for supporting the sky.

This one I give my name.
She tells me
that the song of the all-night rain
will curve the rooftree into the keel
of a brownoak boat.   That sky
will clothe us in light
come dawn
in another country.

Place of Departure

The artists are dying here.
I saw a girl on the wharf singing in Latin
while the wind picked crystalline fragments
out of her breath and threw their iciness
in a white net around her;
it made us all shiver as we passed.
Later, someone placed two silver coins from her bowl
over her shuttered eyes.

The long-haired boy with thin fingers
crouches to play his guitar.
He is leaking roses all over the pavement.
The hole in his stomach has broken its hinge
and swung outward, releasing
this warm perfumed tumble of bloody red flowers and fire.
In this cold winter soon he'll be part of the dust.
The boy's child sits quietly,
holding a rose to his lips like a kiss.

In a tower of light and stone standing watching the tide
the painter cries like a wolf. As he howls
he paints a part of himself into the seascape,
each note a new colour; already only a life-line of charcoal
anchors his heart to his hand. Night after night, stars
peek more dangerously through the vaulted green spaces
enclosed by his floating ribs.

The sculptor is struggling to fashion a double
from a grey *papier mâché* of forms and begging letters.
Trying to train this pseudo-self
to learn the right alphabet, hit the right keys, still
she is haunted by horses of bronze lashing thunder
in and out of the breakers. She weeps for sand-foals
spindly as armature, failing to breathe in the dawn.

A woman in the single kiosk offering future
told me that last month three dancers froze in snow.
Their tableau was a word no longer written.
She was closing shop, moving her zodiac on,
away from the greasy brine lapping the harbour.
See there, she said, giving a spit and a nod sideways
to a long low building the colour of ash.
That's where they straighten them out,
make them useful. Leastways,
those that don't slip away to the quay through the shadows
on the nights when the boats sail West.

Walking back to you, salt is on my face and eyelids.
I know we must leave on the late tide before all fire is frozen
inside our fingers and hearts
so I bring news of sailings and the hour to catch the wind.

Tonight these long straight roads lie bleached and polished
under tungsten, all the malls and restaurants are glittering;
down in the subway, a cleaner idles his broom through a spill
of brown petals, small change, drops of viridian
and sweeps them into the dirt-filled hairline cracks of the city
where they fall like seeds and go on falling into the future.

Written in the Charts

Today the sea is quiet. Winter can be like this,
a silver cloak over foul weather,
softness as of white wolverine in the air.

Our engines are mute, energy in stasis;
the sails whisper and rub,
fret like ghost palms against stark limbs,
pale December skins flickering
with oblique snakes of water-shadow.

Islands break the horizon's steel grey ruler
as they curve into vision
make frosted leaps, heaving themselves out,
their blurred edges frilled with turquoise,
ridgeback bones set with towers of glass;
some so fragile that I wonder
if they die in gales, if they give up
the lifethread that hangs frail
as blue nightmoth migration.
Some islands shiver deceitfully in this light, as
unattended they swim beyond us. Others
are raven-black mountains with no ways of ascent.

I have a map of names and possibilities.
Eastwards is the Island of Four Revolving Doors,
a castle cultured from copper and brass,
if that was our destination. South
an island of red water that runs like blood
into its cup. Once it housed seals, pissmires,
griffins carved from sea-rolled amber.
It has been made safe, they say, for summer;
the beaches stretch hot and unendurably golden.

There have been no seabirds now for seven days:
water is clear, pure as empty glass.
We watch the sensors for those invisibles
we must avoid, uneasy needles
sweeping the screens in glittering arcs,
as if they charted the luminous moony face of Time
with all its smooth oceans, fathomed craters:
Tranquillitatis, Crisieum, Palus Epidemiarum.

We argue about our destination. We conflict
and I cry out, slam my hand against the cabin wall
so the whole ship tremors nervously.
Beyond the porthole, stars I have never seen before
begin to burn a vivid zodiac of fire;
all night, I try to read our future in the charts.

In the Mouth of the Shell

Even on still nights I could slide into the blue
allow the taking wave to coil around my body like love
and on some grey grainy days I forget to wind the silver wire
between love's spindle and my wrist and it reels out
like a seeking-snake, all electricity and violence,
trip-wire, live-wire, loose-end. So tonight when the wind
is a wildness cancelling the screens into colourless storms,
cutting all language, rendered our fantasies blind
I have nothing to bind me; no ropes of words, no rings.

       – but I am tissues and spangles, a one sided smile
you are a tree root hauled to the light, chose me,
chose me over your tasks and old letters –

I always thought my hands spoke – or my eyes;
all too big; volumes, loud, the way I cry,
my hands red hams, fists swollen by water.
If you hear me, you recognise the drums of danger,
hunch into your own weather. Sometimes
you tie me to the mast and stop your ears to save us both
but tonight I am certainly dumb.

Love or die the ocean whispers as I lift the shell to listen,
love or die. Translated through the salty odours
of this hollow milkwhite mouth the words fizz
and hum inside my head; I hear the Wind prowling,
murmuring his restless songs and I allow him to enter,
lie naked, knowing coldness silking over my skin
in a sequence of kissing tide. Wind now will bring
my demon lover – or you, coming in gleaming
from the dark night sea and the long swim of desire;
wordless, with common language, eye and hand
opening the book of tongues, making the sign
of one word, over and over and over and over and over.

Island of Snow

Even under skins of ermine and ivory rabbit
cold gnaws at the edge of ourselves
and we could fall
    fuse with the snow that lies
   deathwhite on the land's face –
     powder masking the cracks.

    Cat-ice claws the old grass
where wind has left its airy creatures caught
beneath the surface of flood wavelets.
    My sympathetic coat trails and shivers.

We are both without colour or cave
on this headland where each habitation
is wide to wind's court of owls.
We are curious strangers, striding staring
at ruins, the echoes of hearth's without embers.

Birdhouse

Bird voices numb to frost
song-silent, stars wrapping the branches
in glitter and everywhere ice

and birdhouses begin to crack, their fragile walls
make small plaintive cries
and I am homeless
>   *Birdhouse of turquoise, let me in let me in*
>   *I am starving cold, blue with cold.*
>   *Birdhouse of straw*
>   *I burn in the freezing strafe of this east wind*
>   *Birdhouse of jade reed, red fern let me curl*
>   *in your hold*

The little houses are crying and cracking like eggs
and the winter fist is squeezing and laughing
I am far too young
for this night of broken houses and ice stars
let me in, let me in —

False Summerlands

Mica scattered over the horizon quickens us:
an island catching fire –

Coloured lights are burning out one by one
across the winter, advertising only lonliness
without grace. Arianrhod's Castle
is made with the broken spars of ballrooms,
tinsel spins of slot machines and mirrorballs
that splinter ecstasy easy as a grain of dirty sand.

Rocks are barbed with glass so cormorants
have bleeding feet, grass is tinctured with little fires,
tide scummed with the detritus of another careless season.
In this frozen morning, a blare of music
hangs like an swarm of bees within the ghostly smell
of barbecue and stale swilled beer.

And is this the Summerlands?
The island of the West where the dead
may find their love again, listening to larks
singing glory into stone and sun breathing rapture
through the mouths of flowers?
Is this how we have made our heaven?

Selky

As I stood at the mirror she swam in behind me
slid her salt hands over my breasts
and into my hollow centre.

She shrugged me over her self, pulled the tissue moon
of my white paper face tight over her cheekbones
so she stared out through my eyes.

We are not dissimilar – both deep-sea-gazed,
and how could you know she is here, under my skin
in the limb and the blood, in the flood of me.

I have become a liquid thing, leak brine
at sudden inappropriate times, bleed like a tide
when I hack at her arms and fingers.

Her hunger is a potent chanting smokiness
that alters everything. She grows and becomes in me:
beached blubber queen, fat lady, lardy thighs –

And you - you are quicksilver and gone.
She made you a mask on a stick, a murmur.
Such clever hands we have, such claws.

Blue

North wind washing the morning sky and sea into blue
your eyes blue as some polar harbour
where seals sing like women.

Haze in silvery glitter is running the lip
of each small wave.
You recognised wave-arpeggios, smile, tilt you head
to listen to music beyond me
>
> *but I have to describe the scaley finny things*
> *that are pressing their wet hands to the sides of the boat*
> *their sucking slapping sounds coming close, close*
> *I am afraid of their bite and weight*
> *and the dark bulk of endless heaving water*
> *cliffs and chasms, roaring mouths and words*
> *coming out of black memories under the ice –*

I crouch in the cabin and you come in wet
with your hair a diamond hood and say
    Dolphins!   and I want to believe:
the myth of dolphins ignites tiny flames in your eyes
and I can see their blue leaping

will they be there for me? Or only fading light
a dull day in winter, the numbing sea.
If you stay here to coax and caress me out
this sealight will fade with the dolphins
but I want you to stay, to alter the dark in here
with your blue stare, your presence my consolation

> *and I want you to turn away so I can grieve*
> *for your lack of love and not move, not move.*

If I let go my hold on this table and chair, step out
on the thin uncertain veneer between here and there
I will be so naked not even you will exist
in the blue space between Ocean and I.

Black Moon

Black night, black sea
    no stars to guide me

a wind is coming in from the north
to carry me lightly as a cargo of autumn leaves
    I am without gifts or energy, leaf-
        child in me, frail as parchment

and every towering wave is a hand that moves
the distance, each gull is a voice that speaks
of clinical news: a woman in starched white
rows over the polished floor, clicking the tide
    marking the spaces between us.

    Black moon
no true horizon: only the child in the reed boat
gliding between the roots of watercress and violet
    on the river under the ocean

watching the empty silence with wide dry eyes.

Selkies

In caves and crannies, under thrift and sea-campion
the women are seeking their lost children.
Round and round every rock they go
dabbing their butterfly nets at shadows –
the nets are torn full of holes
        and the women's harsh calls pierce
           the wind and water silence.

The children are in the water
under the wave where the women can't look.
They are swimming like small seals
but their mouths are open, saying O

O mouths open for milk, for lullabies, for kisses.

The women are frantic, turning and staring,
their hair flying into their eyes, their limbs
heavy as cut trees. The wind stokes them with
      one hand of compassion and one hand edged
     with the sharp silver of memory;
         the wind's shifting voice
        has all the history of whispering.

Too many bodies swimming like seals in the blue.
Small and rounded, the blue filters through
and they have no edge between water and bone
they are blue, salt, seal-baby-ghosts
on the sea's blue coil, faces small, white, bruised,
      mouths open in O

          O Mother
     their eyes are brimming with salt,   blue
      spilling the ocean out of themselves.

Names never spoken become songs in the wind's speech
My Twelve-week Child, My Red-Cell, My River-child,
My Murder, My Bird-Without-Breath

O Mother Ocean   the women are beating the sea
with their torn nets and their hand's helplessness.
They weep in a clamour calling white birds
with their wings of silk who come wheeling and diving
into the baby-shoals, collecting their souls
and flying home.

And the women go on
somehow   not turning to stone
under the sky where the seabirds gleam and weave
they go on   searching
    for the perfect comfort and fit
   of their own sealskins, hidden somewhere
     at the edge, on the shore,
in the black liminal space of caves or crannies.

Island of Spoken Hours

This also is familiar, this small river island
of bare hawthorn and hazel.
We found each other here, half-drowned by winter floods
we pulled the island over our frozen bodies
like a second skin, slept, murmuring our histories.

Water lisps to the shore in circles.
Something is stated by the reaching rings:
do they lose their sense, like Chinese whispers
as they reach further and further or do they
deepen, sonorous as waves under weather's advent,
thunderous, in their repetition, as a Book of Hours?
Their rippling contains the calm plover on the stone,
the kingfishers's arrow. Lie down with me here
on the frosted bank, place your hand on my heart.

Listen.
For all the tricks of the wind distorting the surface,
still the water remembers: spirit, heartbeat, love.
The river will tell us our names again and again:
the first wave is a true version, the ninth a prophecy.

Horse and the Word

The Horse has a Word
to tell me

could be something like
Opensesame or *Ali'kazar*
a rune of the lips
a steamy breathiness

Horse knows that I already
know the word

I may even remember its origin
in the beat of dakini feet on stone
the awkward huge cry of herons

Horse holds out her body as a gift
she is nervous
delicate in silver shoes
her breath hangs like smoke
in the frosty air as if
she is fuelled by fire

she is waiting for me
to get close enough.

Feng Shui for Nightmares

I pussyfoot about the Halls of Dis in my bright kimono
sashed with cherry trees, fans and edible bamboo.
I am using this small hour to search for a particular shadow
amongst those that inhabit this place, scuttling
under the longcase clocks, or leaning out
from behind the black oak cabinets so overcrowded with bijoux
and elegant porcelain bequeathed by Victorian ancestors,
China-lovers; then by my Father in the fifties.

The Nightmare's shadow bulks over many walls.
I smell her presence in the sweet reek of sweat
and there's dungcakes and piss in it and foam
flecking hide in a saltspray as if
she were one of Neptune's own and maybe she is
with her sharp head-splitting hooves that skim at me
like stones over water or memories.

Her shadows have family fingers and threats and they menace
from dim corners like shars, so I answer back weakly,
enumerating the knots of my Chinese motifs. I am glad
that my my stepping is safely encased in red embroidered slippers
signed in sequins for heavenly beatitude.
My footsteps mince and drag but there is a beat to them;
my arrhythmia plays piano to drum as I go northwest
towards *Chien*.

               Soon I will come to the mare.
She may be drinking water from the silver-plated flagon
in the master-bedroom or quietly grazing from a tapestry,
she could be already wrapped in sheets of snowy lace and linen.
You might not think that I am dressed for riding
wearing only this thin robe of blossomed cotton cherry
with no defensive leathers or vicuna on me
but I have learned to meet her softly, bring her out of the dark
gently as Kuan Yin walking with a child.

It has taken years to understand how to assemble magnolias,
mirrors and sugar pills, how to give the gift of sweetgrass reins
delicate as love. Now I collect the mare, ride slow dressage,
let her dance. Her muscles held within my hand are lightning bolts,
the sea is roaring, filling out my skirts with its fierce clean white.
Seven directions of the *Pa-Kua* open out before us like lotus petals
and we chose *Tui*, the Joyful. Breathe.

Going Under

Already at the brink he could have gone in storm, raging
under its electric dagger, naked, phosphorous, blue,
his body flickering into conflict, responding
to commands of Thunder, the God rising in his blood,
streaming out beyond the known cone of himself.
In storm, he would have descended violently into water,
bull-roaring helplessly at annihilation, bruising fists
hammering the cold green gates of Manannan's palaces
until the locks of dulse and wrack broke open
and he jack-knifed through
the undertow wound round his body like a guiding rope.

Or did he chose a day like this – a grace of light
silver on the tide. He could have walked into the river
at the estuary's long loop
between tiers of blazing gorse where larks spiral out to heaven
and mossy boulders hold the empty cave of ram's white ribs
as an archway for the bees.   Going out with the tide
he could have followed the wake of blue-legged swans
stately as burial barges, his hands grown frond-like
trailing nets through the river's speed, spread toes
tender to the peaty ooze, his face
still within the realm of real time; one white feather
coming back to him, and passing.

Only water was open for him now he was deafened to earth,
to air. At the edge, the waves' cadenza
drowned the shrill piping of oyster catchers;
only the seagull's screams reached him, and tore him.
Black-plumed cormorants flew a line of nine
and one stood as an angel pointing deep
as the Sea took him, hushing his cries, soothing
the salt from his skin, his eyes.

                         Going under
that glittery silver light became milky and he could sleep.
Gently then his memoried cells unfolded
like paper water-flowers finding their release.

Afterwards he would only shrug and say some luck of wind
had turned a sail towards him.
He was changed of course. I saw that his hands had opened out
and he held his palms wide as if both receiving and letting go,
whatever the weather. I would say he prospered, late in life,
began to paint, loved again, grew tangerines.

Dreaming the Well

High in the white air above me a lammergeier wheels
and searches. He is small as the flies that circle
insistently, drunk on the scent of my sweat
as I scrape scrape at the sand, my hands bloodied
in late sunlight that makes this a Red Desert today
last rays adding a blood-sheen
so I see that I rode here on a Firehorse, my old roan,
carnelian in this lapping crackling light.
So I scrape and scrape.

The sand is rough and precious, gold serrations,
skivers of silvery amethyst, abrasions of quartz.
It would all melt into goblets or lamps,
stretch into honeypanes for windows into the desert.
I could make earrings of citrine
let them hang in my ears like a crystal set tuned to
the dry yellow secrets of desert fox or sand-spirits.

So I scrape and scrape. Until something comes alive
under my hand and the last grains of sand
I blow from a well's sheer bright surface.
In the tightly held distance
the shaft circles blackness like index finger and thumb
magically signing that this water-eye watching me
is the mirror of night, the first rim of space.

In my cat form I climb down, using my claws,
headfirst with my sensitive whiskers shivering.
Inch by inch out of the desert into this blue black
tunnel of water and air that smells salt, fresh, curious.
In my cat form I scoop the stars like fish.

I'll be the ship's cat when I reach her:
dizzy and windblown up in the Crow's Nest
I'll be the first to sight land
and the first to step ashore.

Storm

Thunder stalking –
    our dreams tremble and flicker
as the bed unmoors and moves downstream –

      already my lungs struggle like salmon
          my breath hisses with drowning –

but tonight the weather turns away –

North Wind is a witch's broom scouring
the ceilings of all four directions
    and this is home
this black dome hung with fire-studs and chandeliers
    Draco taking the part of a house snake
        scaled in beryl
Leo's paw flexing in remnants of cloud-angora
his squint eyes lighting the wave.

I use a book of poems as an oar
slicing the water into sheaves of light and shadow
my paper charts dissolve in salt –

a bracelet moon comes to starboard:
tomorrow's islands wait like grails.

The Light Falling

And if there's anything I'd go back for
it is moonlight and love in half-shadowed grass
under black tree's fine seine nets
sifting summer's night, sky green-turquoise still
at an improbable hour of mackerel cirrus
with so few floating stars
that no minatory silver-studded dragon or
chancy sea-goat can approach us as we lie together.

Nor any messengers, coming in a thunder-race
from the scales of Libra, holding dawn in one hand
like a shawl and in the other the sombre warnings
of crow's shaky linear flight.

I have never – could never have – loved enough
in moonlight: that tender pearly silk of moonlight
on our skin, the wonder of it
as you enter me. Your face and the moon above
a mystery, that this is so – love
and its phases. As if you pour the moon into me
because I open, call your name to come.

And in this makeshift harbour,
in this uneasy pull of tides, our shared bed
is sometimes dangerous as a raft, slight as a yacht
too small for radar, a catamaran adrift. Once
I dreamed a great galleon with every sail and spar
lit gold as it sailed through space, its round nimbus
full and shining as a moon. Such dreams
nurture me. Even the old crescent drowned like an eel
in the street's airy lace will make me pause, look at you
again, remembering that at the edge
light always falls towards an undiscovered ocean.

Clear Water

Clear water: coming into this island the bay is a cleft of blue,
a sky-bowl, cobalt and calm. Seals watch us with curious eyes,
sun is their sensory teacher and they roll and bask,
like women they loll and murmer. Our voices drop into softness
with the cessation of the wind and the warmth
of this morning's new sun; frost still lingers in shadow's mauve.

Sometimes I forget we are making this journey together.
I'm too close to the mirror that watches my body, my years
click into silence, my owl-fears, my dresses that fall into dust.

But we have sailed between green icebergs whose coldness
burned our bones, so we were ice-bound, slow and clumsy
with each other, our gestures like little knives; the weight of ice
on our eyelids blurring our dreams.

I have seen you change. I hold out my hands full of memories
but they run through my fingers like this salt blue water.
This was one moment ago, the boy and the baby,
what happened to us, what happened to you?
You are becoming lined and grey-feathered like me
and the place between us is wider now
but so silver the light of it, lying across the horizon.
Something happened while we slept. We passed sirens,
mazy islands, dangers and illusions, and we grew older, came
eventually to this clear water; watching each other with wary love

Haven

In the House of the Sun the moon is tilted onto a table
silver laid for a feast.

We walk and I have to tell you stories.
Nothing that happen to me has meaning
unless I relate it back to you
      (this is part of the dream)

sometimes it is in argument, sometimes
it is in the form of a found birdwing
or a drop of water, crystal stud
in my kiss.

The animal dream comes warm-breathed
and clovery, yellow eyes calm.
You run your hand over the guard hairs
on the hound's back
and feel knowledge shiver under your fingers.
Tonight you will sit alone in the straw
watching the mother give birth

while the cat and I will silently watch
the disseminating moon. Dance maybe.

In this tall panelled room
the dark wood and the books dream
we both float bookishly, studious
up over the soft armchairs, between the mullions.
Stories are wound between our hands
like mohair, spidery glinting filaments.

And the children of children run in flaring and fizzing
and out again, leaving a trace in the ash
a sudden warmth.

The sea changes.
I swear if I put my hands in this new water
they would grow warm from the fires collected
in this sunlit wave under the wave
on the sun-path to shore.

The Third Deer

The first deer that walked into the town was shot.
Someone said it was blind and crazy, why else
would it have come in that dark earliness,
stepping down the long steep hill
between the shuttered Georgian hotels and bars?
Frail as first snowfall she came, white on white
moving with precise and delicate hooves
over the frosted glittering tarmac, across
the hoar-frosted park where the blue cedars
stood watching, their tiered white lace frozen
breathless as fretted stone. Quietly, she came
over the ice on the round pond deep as a mirror,
past the overflow's quiver of ice spears and arrows,
into the heart of the town, into the vapours
and acid lights, and into the fire of careless people.

The second deer chose her time more carefully,
came in the small hours and not on a Saturday.
Came warily through moonlit streets like a white ghost
out of the valley; a white lady, a story.
She spooked the cats and set dogs howling like wolves
or they became wolves briefly, howling
the skin-chill senses of moon and wild and deer.
This one was seen three times – Or was smoke
in a distant garden, a renegade deerhound
bleached by tungsten, a trick of mist. No one
believed in her and she could not stay.

Disappearing, she left uneasy prints like tear-tracks
over the dreams of the town, made the people sweat
and cry out in their sleep and wake with a longing
for something unknown, but lost.

The third time Deer chose a different path
and I could have so easily missed her
because she was a Spirit-Deer and came in the form
of the frosted swan on the lake and as the barn owl
flying towards me with my own young face.
She came through the red fumed absence of stars
as a white-tailed star falling through true darkness
her breath warming the frost ferns on the glass
one breath at a time, slowly –
a song in a woman's voice making a misted circle
until I rubbed it clear and gazed out through her eyes
at the other land – *at the edge*
the grace of air and bright waves: such wide space
describing the infinite distance of light beyond me
and within me –
so the pale town fell away like the scales
of an outworn snakeskin and Deer's song took us home.

ALSO AVAILABLE FROM STRIDE

Sheen Peter Redgrove

Peter Redgrove's last book is one of his most vital with its vivid cluster of images, burst of ideas and bubbling energy. Redgrove both invents the wonderful and sees it in the everyday. He is a poet who prodigiously celebrates and in *Sheen* he is as inspirational and generous as ever. He reveals and creates. He illuminates, juxtaposes; is the scientist of the surreal. He never wears gloves; he touches everything with his own fingers. We feel it all with the same intensity as he does, delicate and raw. He opens doors by the way he looks at what is round him, books, gardens, water, those he loves. In the poignant 'Spiritualism Garden' he pictures himself 'eating on the edge of death', yet in these poems the pulse is as strong as ever; the images as brilliant and original, the gift as abundant; warm, fecund, it germinates still.

'To dip into his work is to receive the gift of magic, and once you're inside you may wish, like me, never to come out.'   – Jeremy Reed, *Temenos*

ISBN 1 900152 87 8   £10.00

Lady Chapel Sarah Law

The Lady Chapel houses a variety of saints and sinners. Women mystics – from the medieval Hildegard of Bingen to the longsuffering Mrs Yeats – step forward and expand our ideas of the divine. Other voices, male and female, respond by exploring conditions of intimacy or isolation. The collection ends with a sequence of yoga poems, where language is stretched along with the body, offering new perspectives on our unpredictable world.

'This is one of the most surprising and exciting collections I have read in a good while.' – George Szirtes

ISBN 1 900152 88 6   £8.50

These books are available, post free, from
STRIDE, 11 SYLVAN ROAD, EXETER, DEVON EX4 6EW, ENGLAND